MW01152456

Why We Eat Fried Peanuts

Mèng (梦- *muhng*) means
"dream" in Mandarin.

Zed Zha

Illustrated by
Sian James

龙馬精神

"Now it feels like the New Year celebration is really starting!" Dad said, picking up a freshly fried peanut with his chopsticks. "Mèng, have one!"

太奶奶
tài nǎi nai
⬥⬥⬥⬥⬥
tie-nigh-nigh
great-grandmother

"**Yum!** Dad, why do we eat fried peanuts every New Year?"

"When I was a little boy, your *tài nǎi nai* always told me to eat more peanuts so I could live long and be strong. And everyone always listened to your tài nǎi nai!"

"Tài Nǎi Nai was the most *rè xīn* person in the world, and she always helped everyone," Dad said. "Every generation–Tài Nǎi Nai's siblings, my dad, me, and you–we all learn from her kindness and bravery!"

"Is that why I have to kneel and talk to Tài Nǎi Nai by her grave every Tomb-Sweeping Day?"

热心
rè xīn
◇◇◇◇◇
juh-sin
warmhearted

"Qingming Festival, or *Qīng Míng Jié*, is when we sweep the tombs of our loved ones who have died to honor them. When we kneel to talk to our ancestors, they bless us and pray for our good fortune," Dad explained.

"So Tài Nǎi Nai is always looking after us?" Mèng asked with excitement.

"In our culture we believe the spirit lives on after death. This is why we don't live just for ourselves. We represent our ancestors–like your tài nǎi nai, our family legend–in everything we do."

清明节
Qīng Míng Jié

Ching-ming-jeh
Qingming Festival

"Many years ago, your tài nǎi nai took care of the family and was the head of the household. She was great at sewing clothes, making sure that the family had everything they needed for meals, and that all the chores and errands were done. When she spoke, everyone listened," Dad said with pride.

故事
gù shì
◇◇◇◇◇
gu-shir
story

"**Wow.** I want to be like Tài Nǎi Nai! What was her name?"

"Well . . . we don't know."

"You don't know your grandma's name?"

"Family histories didn't always include women's names. We lost your tài nǎi nai's name, but we will always remember her *gù shì*."

In early winter of 1926, Tài Nǎi Nai was taking a walk in her neighborhood in Beijing, a big city in China. She passed a pregnant woman who looked a few years younger than her.

姑娘
gū niáng

◇◇◇◇◇

goon-yah
young woman

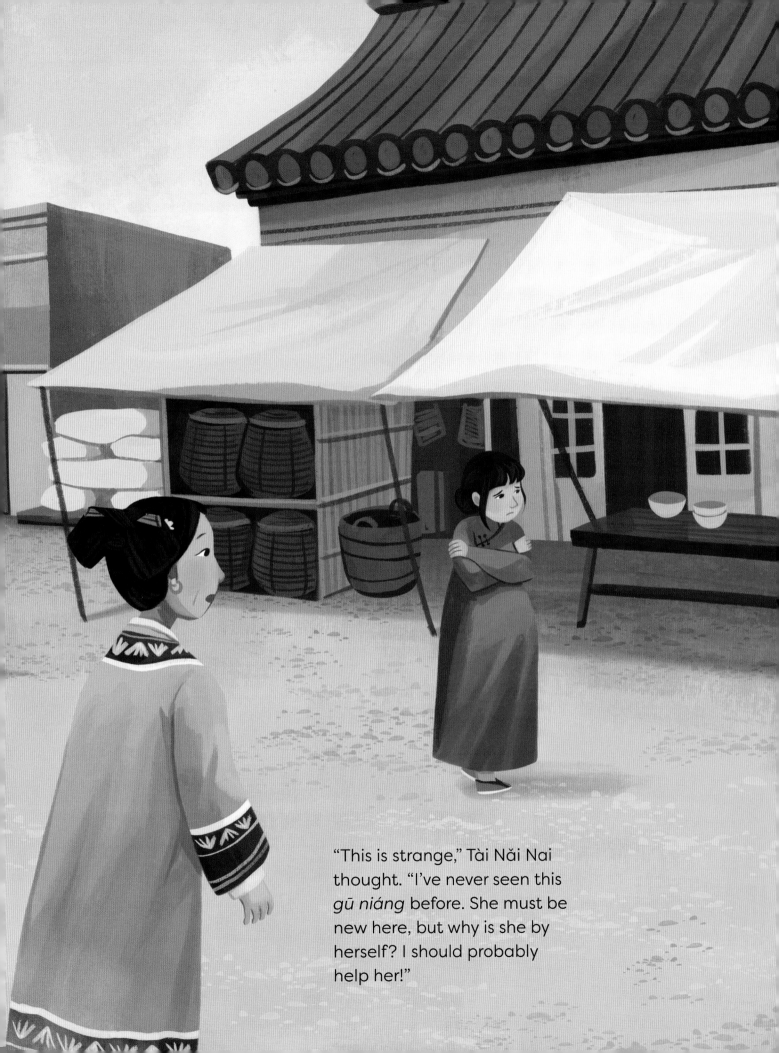

"This is strange," Tài Nǎi Nai thought. "I've never seen this *gū niáng* before. She must be new here, but why is she by herself? I should probably help her!"

"Have you eaten today?" Tài Nǎi Nai asked the woman warmly.

The woman didn't answer and tried to walk away.

"When are you due to give birth?" Tài Nǎi Nai asked, following. "Can I help you?"

"I don't need *bāng zhù*!" said the woman before running away.

帮助
bāng zhù
◇◇◇◇◇
bon-ju
help

"Something doesn't feel right about this,"
Tài Năi Nai thought. "I must find her!"

Over the next few days, Tài Năi Nai took longer
walks, going to different places around the city
to look for the woman.

One day, she wandered into a *hú tòng* she had
never been to before and spotted one house
with an open gate.

"How odd",
thought Tài Năi Nai.

胡同

hú tòng

◇◇◇◇◇

who-tong

small alley

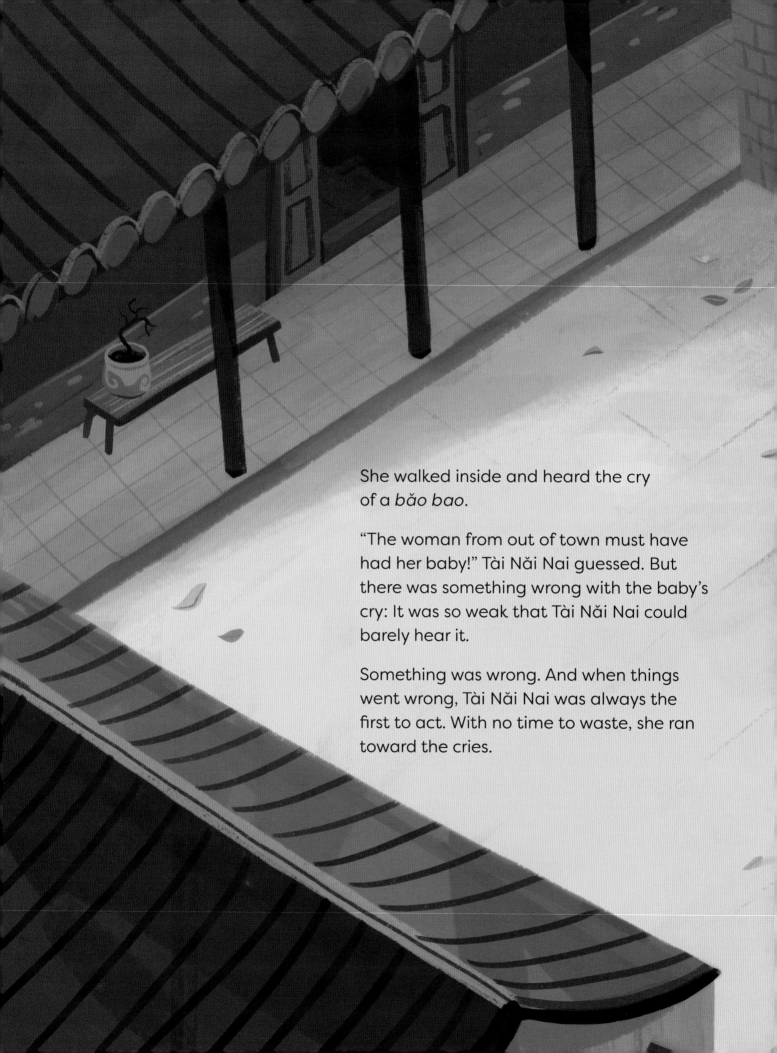

She walked inside and heard the cry of a *bǎo bao*.

"The woman from out of town must have had her baby!" Tài Nǎi Nai guessed. But there was something wrong with the baby's cry: It was so weak that Tài Nǎi Nai could barely hear it.

Something was wrong. And when things went wrong, Tài Nǎi Nai was always the first to act. With no time to waste, she ran toward the cries.

宝宝
bǎo bao

✦✦✦✦✦

bao-bao

baby

Tài Nǎi Nai followed the cries to the living room and found the baby, cold and not being cared for. She quickly wrapped the baby in a warm blanket.

Holding the baby tight, Tài Nǎi Nai looked for the *mǔ qīn*, who was crying in the corner.

"**Shh,** good bǎo bao."

母亲
mǔ qīn
◇◇◇◇◇
moo-chin
mother

"**Wait!**" Mèng stopped eating her peanuts. "Why wasn't the mom taking care of the baby? That's so cruel!"

Dad shook his head. "She was not cruel. This was a different time, and a war was about to start. The woman's husband was called away to be a soldier. She couldn't afford to raise a child by herself. She had no choice," Dad explained gently.

"**Wow.** We are so *xìng yùn* today," Mèng said.

招財進寶

幸运
xìng yùn
◇◇◇◇◇
shing-yoon
lucky

Tài Nǎi Nai was determined to save the baby.
So, she did something she had only done for her
ancestors during Qingming Festival: She kneeled
on the floor.

"I'm from a good
family. Please let
me take the baby
home and care
for him."

The woman knew that kneeling was a special way to show *zūn zhòng*, so when she saw this, she knew Tài Nǎi Nai's offer was a serious one and agreed.

尊重
zūn zhòng
◇◇◇◇◇
zuen-joan
respect

Tài Nǎi Nai took the baby back to her family and nicknamed him Little Peanut. She hoped that he would take after the hardy *huā shēng* plant and get strong and healthy in his new life.

Little Peanut lived in a happy home as one of Tài Nǎi Nai's children. When he grew up, he became an engineer and enjoyed playing the èr hú, a Chinese musical instrument. Little Peanut was the life of the party wherever he went!

花生
huā shēng
◇◇◇◇◇
huhwa-shung
peanut

"And your great-uncle, Little Peanut, is now ninety-nine years old!" exclaimed Dad. "Why do you think Tài Nǎi Nai always told me to eat more peanuts? A small snack can have a big meaning and can be an everyday reminder of our *zhòng yào* family legends."

重要
zhòng yào
◇◇◇◇◇
joan-yao
important

"It's too bad we don't know Tài Nǎi Nai's name," Mèng sighed.

"She was known for her *shàn liáng*, so her name became Kindness," Dad said. "And as we celebrate Lunar New Year, we remember Tài Nǎi Nai's story and show kindness in our own lives each day."

善良
shàn liáng
◇◇◇◇◇
shan-liyong
kindness

Learn about important moments in Chinese history and culture!

What language is spoken in this story?

The language characters in this story represent the Mandarin spoken in northern China. Southern China may call people by different names, like zǔ nǎi nai instead of tài nǎi nai, for example. Pinyin is the official spelling system used in China to help people pronounce the characters. The Chinese language doesn't have an alphabet; the characters represent meanings, not sounds. So pinyin was adopted in 1958 to help describe the sounds of Mandarin Chinese using the Roman (or Latin) alphabet.

What is Lunar New Year?

Also called Spring Festival or Chinese New Year, this is a holiday to welcome the beginning of a new year according to the lunar calendar. No matter where we are in the world, everyone travels home to have a 团圆饭 (tuán yuán fàn), a reunion dinner, with the entire family.

Why are great-grandmothers and their stories important?

The Chinese tradition teaches that our ancestry is as important as the sky we live under and the earth we walk on. 天地父母 (tiān dì fù mǔ) is a common saying in Chinese that literally translates into Sky, Earth, Father, and Mother, showing how important our families are.

Why are peanuts a special treat?

Peanuts have many lucky meanings in Chinese culture. Because each shell contains multiple nuts, peanuts represent prosperity. They are also called longevity fruits, which mean good health and lasting youth for those who eat them.

Why did Tài Nǎi Nai ask about eating before she even said hello?

Food culture is so important to northern Chinese people that neighbors and friends often greet each other this way.

What is Qingming Festival?

This is a day when people pay respect to their ancestors by sweeping dirt away from their loved ones' tombs, bringing gifts, and kneeling to speak to them. The festival happens on the fifteenth day after the spring equinox and usually falls in April.

What is a hú tòng?

In northern China, a hú tòng is a narrow alley formed by two rows of houses. A group of hú tòngs make a neighborhood. Today many hú tòngs have been replaced by roads and large buildings, but some are still protected to preserve the culture.

Why do Chinese people take kneeling in front of others so seriously?

In Chinese culture, to kneel and put your head on the ground represents the most respect you can pay to someone. "There is gold under each man's knees" is a Chinese saying which means kneeling is an action as precious as gold—something you don't give away lightly!

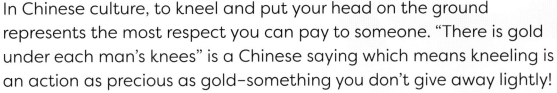

Why do some Chinese parents give their children nicknames that are fruits, plants, or animals?

These names reflect the family's wish for the child to have a simple and easy life like the everyday things around us, and to grow up strong and healthy.

What does the èr hú look and sound like?

This is a two-stringed traditional Chinese musical instrument with a small sound box with strings that you play with a bow, like a violin. The èr hú also sounds a bit like a violin, but the tone is more high pitched.

How to Make Fried Peanuts

◆ **Makes 6 servings** ◆

Peanuts are a symbol of long life, youth, unity, and prosperity. As a *Nóng Lì Xīn Nián* snack, peanuts are often served without their shells. There are many ways to cook peanuts and the flavors come in many varieties, from sweet to savory. Fried peanuts can often be found in Chinese restaurants as side dishes with pots of tea, and of course, on the Lunar New Year Eve dinner table in Chinese American homes.

IMPORTANT! Always work with an adult when handling hot oil, and wear oven mitts or use potholders when picking up a hot pan!

农历新年
Nóng Lì Xīn Nián
◇◇◇◇◇
Non-li-sin-nee-yan
Lunar New Year

Ingredients

6 ounces (170 g) shelled raw red-skin peanuts

Neutral-flavored oil (like canola, vegetable, or peanut oil), enough to cover the peanuts

Sea salt, to taste

Instructions

1. Place the peanuts in a strainer or colander, and rinse under water. Shake off any excess water and drain well. Spread them out in a single layer on paper towels or dish towels to air-dry for at least 30 minutes.

2. In a clean wok or a wide, deep pan, add the air-dried peanuts and enough oil to just cover the peanuts. Then turn on the heat to medium low. Gently and slowly push the peanuts around with a spatula or a spoon to heat them evenly and prevent burning. (You must use cold oil and low heat to start, and use low heat throughout the whole frying process. Don't rush the process, or the peanuts will quickly burn.)

3. As the oil heats up slowly, in about 5 minutes, you will first see small bubbles in the oil, then some steam as the moisture in the peanuts cooks off. You may also hear small popping noises (like a much quieter popcorn). Keep slowly pushing the peanuts around in the oil. The peanuts should be done once the pink skin on the peanuts turns a shade darker (like a light reddish-brown) and the popping sounds slow down. Frying time should be around 7 to 12 minutes, depending on the size of the peanuts.

4. Turn off the stove, put a strainer over a heatproof container, and pour the peanuts and oil into it.

5. Spread the peanuts out in a single layer on a baking sheet or plate to cool them quickly. Another quick cooldown method is to put the peanuts in a large stainless-steel bowl and roll them around to disperse the heat quickly so the peanuts can turn crunchy faster. Toss with salt if desired and serve!

TIPS

You'll see small bubbles and a little bit of hot steam coming out of the oil as the moisture in the peanuts is cooked off. This is normal!

The pink skin should be a shade darker after frying. If the pink color deepens too much, it means that the peanuts are overfried.

With an adult, carefully taste the peanuts during frying to see if they are done. Hot peanuts will not be crunchy yet, but you can taste the doneness.

If you are hearing popping noises coming from the peanuts, that means they are done and should be removed from the oil immediately.

Fried peanuts only become crunchy after they are completely cooled, so it's ok if they are still a little soft when hot.

Any leftover peanuts can be stored in an airtight container. You can also mix a few drops of white vinegar into the hot peanuts to keep them from getting stale.

About the Author

Zed Zha is a first-generation immigrant from China and an important voice for change in the AAPI space. A board-certified family physician, Zed actively engages in teaching and research, and her prolific professional writing about patient care with dignity, reproductive autonomy, and social and medical justice has made her a recognized name in Chinese American, immigrant, and advocacy circles. Zed's medical career and patient advocacy for people of color have garnered her a following on social media, but so has her personal writing. As a Chinese American, she is passionate about telling stories about ancestry and traditions. Her introspective, vulnerable, and humorous style of narrative nonfiction shines in her original Tài Nǎi Nai ("great-grandmother") story, on which her first children's book is based. Follow Zed at zedzha.com/join and @DrZedZha on X (Twitter).

About the Illustrator

Sian James has been drawing ever since she could pick up a pencil. Having lived a previous life as an archaeologist, she likes to combine her passions for nature, history, and art to tell stories from the mundane to the magical. She lives in Cambridge, England, with her husband, daughter, and two cats.

© 2025 by Quarto Publishing Group USA Inc.
Text © 2025 by Zed Zha

First published in 2025 by becker&mayer!kids, an imprint of The Quarto Group,
142 West 36th Street, 4th Floor, New York, NY 10018, USA
(212) 779-4972 www.Quarto.com

All rights reserved. No part of this book may be reproduced in any form without written
permission of the copyright owners. All images in this book have been reproduced
with the knowledge and prior consent of the artists concerned, and no responsibility
is accepted by producer, publisher, or printer for any infringement of copyright or
otherwise, arising from the contents of this publication. Every effort has been made to
ensure that credits accurately comply with information supplied. We apologize for any
inaccuracies that may have occurred and will resolve inaccurate or missing information
in a subsequent reprinting of the book.

becker&mayer!kids titles are also available at discount for retail, wholesale,
promotional, and bulk purchase. For details, contact the Special Sales Manager by
email at specialsales@quarto.com or by mail at The Quarto Group, Attn: Special Sales
Manager, 100 Cummings Center Suite 265D, Beverly, MA 01915 USA.

10 9 8 7 6 5 4 3 2 1

ISBN: 978-0-7603-9552-3

Digital edition published in 2025
eISBN: 978-0-7603-9554-7

Library of Congress Control Number: 2024943786

Publisher: Rage Kindelsperger
Creative Director: Laura Drew
Senior Art Director: Marisa Kwek
Managing Editor: Cara Donaldson
Cover and Interior Design: Marisa Kwek
Cover and Interior Illustrations: Sian James

Printed in China

LEXILE

Lexile® 860L

FSC
MIX
Paper | Supporting
responsible forestry
FSC® C016973
www.fsc.org